DUDLEY SCHOOLS
LIBRARY SERVICE

KU-395-636

Schools Library and Information Services

S00000794509

OCTOPUSES

by **Elizabeth R. Johnson**

raintree

a Capstone company — publishers for children

Raintree is an imprint of Capstone Global Library Limited, a company incorporated in England and Wales having its registered office at 264 Banbury Road, Oxford, OX2 7DY – Registered company number: 6695582

www.raintree.co.uk
myorders@raintree.co.uk

Text © Capstone Global Library Limited 2017
The moral rights of the proprietor have been asserted.

All rights reserved. No part of this publication may be reproduced in any form or by any means (including photocopying or storing it in any medium by electronic means and whether or not transiently or incidentally to some other use of this publication) without the written permission of the copyright owner, except in accordance with the provisions of the Copyright, Designs and Patents Act 1988 or under the terms of a licence issued by the Copyright Licensing Agency, Saffron House, 6–10 Kirby Street, London EC1N 8TS (www.cla.co.uk). Applications for the copyright owner's written permission should be addressed to the publisher.

ISBN 978 1 4747 2589 7
20 19 18 17 16
10 9 8 7 6 5 4 3 2 1

British Library Cataloguing in Publication Data
A full catalogue record for this book is available from the British Library.

Editorial Credits
Jaclyn Jaycox, editor; Philippa Jenkins, designer;
Svetlana Zhurkin, media researcher; Gene Bentdahl, production specialist

Photo Credits
iStockphoto: richcarey, cover, 13; Minden Pictures: Colin Marshall, 15; Shutterstock: Andrea Izzotti, 9, littlesam, 19, Photonimo, 7, Rich Carey, back cover, 3, 5, 11, 14, 24, Sphinx Wang, 21, Vittorio Bruno, 17

Design Elements by Shutterstock

Every effort has been made to contact copyright holders of material reproduced in this book. Any omissions will be rectified in subsequent printings if notice is given to the publisher.

All the Internet addresses (URLs) given in this book were valid at the time of going to press. However, due to the dynamic nature of the Internet, some addresses may have changed, or sites may have changed or ceased to exist since publication. While the author and publisher regret any inconvenience this may cause readers, no responsibility for any such changes can be accepted by either the author or the publisher.

DUDLEY SCHOOLS LIBRARY SERVICE	
S00000794509	
£11.99	J594.56
06-Feb-2017	PETERS

Printed and bound in China.

Contents

Life in the ocean

An octopus crawls along the ocean floor. Eight long arms look for food and places to hide. Each of its arms can stretch 9 metres (30 feet)!

Octopuses live in oceans around the world. Most octopuses like warm water. They can live in deep or shallow water.

Up close

There are more than 300 types of octopus. The smallest is less than 2.5 centimetres (1 inch) long. The biggest is 5.5 metres (18 ft) long!

An octopus has a large head.

Its head holds a brain,

a stomach and three hearts.

Octopuses have no bones. They

can squeeze into tiny spaces.

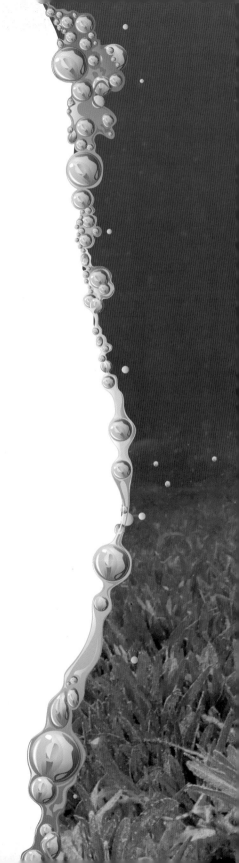

Finding food

Octopus arms are lined with many suckers. Suckers can taste what they touch. The arms reach into holes to find food.

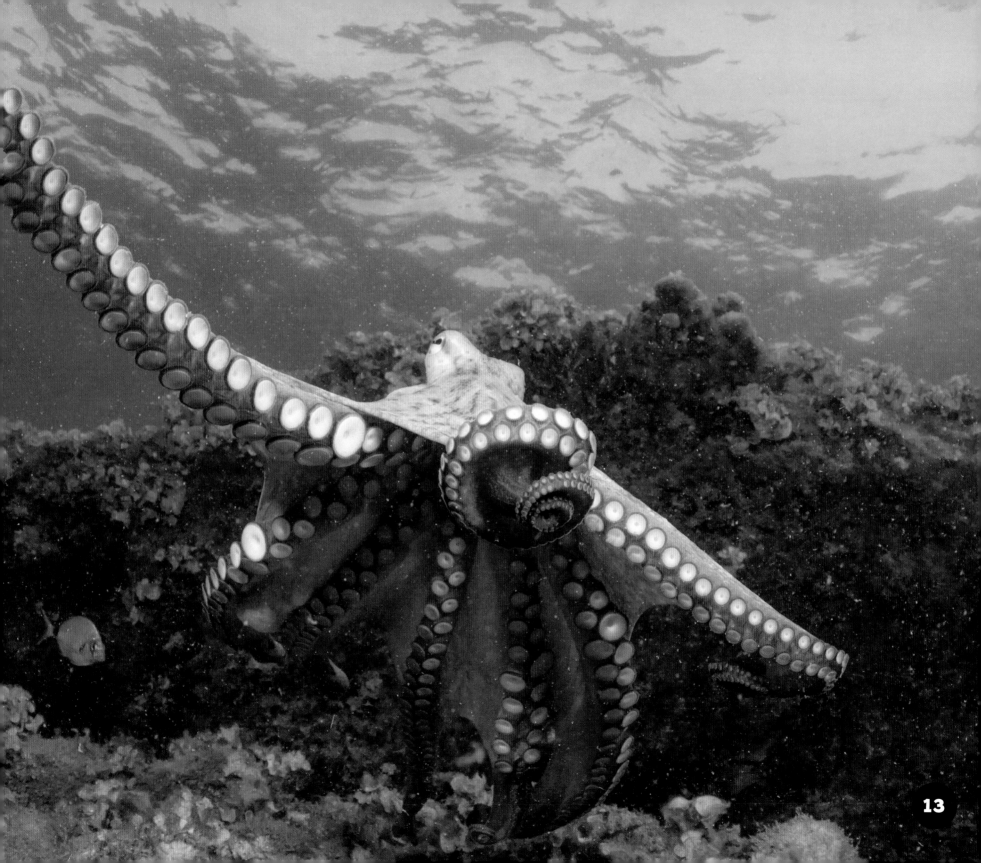

With their long arms, octopuses snatch prey. Their sharp beaks and strong tongues can break hard shells. Octopuses eat crabs, lobsters, shrimp and fish.

Staying safe

When threatened, an octopus
squirts a cloud of ink into
the water. The ink confuses the
predator. Then the octopus
swims away.

Octopuses can camouflage themselves. That means they change colour to blend in with their surroundings. Predators find it hard to see them!

Life cycle

A female octopus lays up to 400,000 eggs. Most baby octopuses hatch in four to six weeks. An octopus lives for about one to two years.

Glossary

beak   horny projecting jaw of animals; an octopus beak looks like a parrot's beak

camouflage   pattern or colour on an animal's skin that helps it to blend in with things around it

hatch   break out of an egg

predator   animal that hunts other animals for food

prey   animal hunted by another animal for food

shallow   not deep

snatch   grab

sucker   soft, flexible part on an animal's body that is used to cling on to something

surroundings   things around something or someone

threatened   put in danger

Read more

First Encyclopedia of Seas and Oceans, Ben Denne (Usborne Publishing, 2011)

Living and Non-Living in the Ocean (Is it Living or Non-Living?) Rebecca Rissman (Raintree, 2014)

Ocean Food Chains (Food Chains and Webs), Angela Royston (Raintree, 2014)

Websites

www.bbc.co.uk/nature/life/Octopus
Discover more about octopuses.

www.dkfindout.com/uk/animals-and-nature/invertebrates/octopuses/
Learn more about octopuses and take a look at a common octopus up close!

Index